"...There is revelation in Browning's suffering prose, in her darkness, and her failures. In her willingness and courage. She is deeply connected to the source of suffering and to the root of our human condition. She is not afraid to look the many elements of our mortal life in the face and to transcend them with fierce belief in the ancient ways."

  —ALAN COOKE, Emmy-winning writer and filmmaker

"L.M. Browning's powerful poetry embodies the archetypal spiritual journey of our times...her impassioned words evoke our longing to unite with the Source that gave rise to the cosmos, the earth, and the depths of our hearts."

  —DREW DELLINGER, author of *Love Letter to the Milky Way*

"Browning's verse is embedded in ancient wisdom,
which springs from the Source, touching us deep in our hearts
and ultimately connecting us with ourselves."
  —MARYAM MAFI, author of *Rumi, Day by Day*

"Browning spins fibers with every word and image that beautifully weave together into a fabric of a sacred landscape. ...Every word is precise and chosen carefully opening our hearts and revealing insights into the truth that lies within...."

  —SANDRA INGERMAN, author of *Soul Retrieval*

"...The essential struggle of the poet is not so much to understand our lives, but to fully experience our aliveness. In reading her work, in sharing her struggle, I cannot but feel a kinship to Browning. But perhaps this is just because all good poets make us feel this way."

  —THEODORE RICHARDS, award-winning author of *Cosmosophia*

Seasons

of Contemplation

A Book of Midnight Meditations

Seasons
of Contemplation

A Book of Midnight Meditations

L.M. Browning

HOMEBOUND
PUBLICATIONS
Independent Publisher of Contemplative Titles
STONINGTON, CONNECTICUT

HOMEBOUND PUBLICATIONS

Seasons of Contemplation
Copyright © 2015 by L.M. Browning

FIRST EDITION TRADE PAPERBACK

ISBN: 978-1-938846-16-8 (pbk)

www.homeboundpublications.com or visit the author at www.lmbrowning.com

Book Designed by Leslie M. Browning
Cover Image by © Subbotina Anna | Shutterstock.com

Library of Congress Cataloging-in-Publication Data

Browning, L. M.
Seasons of contemplation : a book of midnight meditations / by L.M. Browning. -- First Edition.
pages cm
ISBN 978-1-938846-16-8 (pbk.)
1. Meditations. 1. Title.
BL624.2.B765 2015
814'.6--dc23
2015000320

10 9 8 7 6 5 4 3 2 1

Homebound Publications holds a fervor for environmental conservation. Atop
donating a percentage of our annual income to an ecological charity, we are ever-
mindful of our "carbon footprint". Our books are printed on paper with chain of
custody certification from the Forest Stewardship Council, Sustainable Forestry
Initiative, and the Programme for the Endorsement of Forest Certification. This
ensures that, in every step of the process, from the tree to the reader's hands, the
paper our books are printed on has come from sustainably managed forests.

Also by L.M. Browning

Contents

What is Left to Us

An Opening Rumination from the Author

In recent years I've found a deepening fatigue hanging heavy about me. It is an exhaustion that sleep cannot diminish, because the tiredness is not of the body but of the spirit.

I do not know how to give the soul the rest it needs. Life only yields brief moments of quietness, no matter how forcefully I beg it to do otherwise; hardly long enough to take a breath let alone sort through the emptiness that nags me.

No, the years have crashed upon me—waves of hardship driven by unrelenting gales. I know not what God I angered, or from what forsaken corner of the world these ill winds blow, but they come. I have matured in the midst of the eternal storm, and found joy in the transcendence of suffering alone; the pure source of happiness being a myth yet to be proven real.

Life. Is it a course we set, or what we manage to cling to throughout the storm? By my eyes, life is the moments we struggle to realize; the people we fight to reach and stay with; and the home we try to build until at last our arms lose their strength, and we must give ourselves over to that place the wind has ever-driven us to go.

I know this fatigue will not be quenched by railing against the forces beyond my control. That only robs me of more strength. No, all I can do is feed the soul as I do the body, in an effort to keep my spirit hearty. Not with bread, but with quietness and the fruits of solitude.

I sit by the fire, bound in an old blanket, this body held together only by the will to remain beside those I love. Basking in the warmth of those companions filling my house, and the life we have managed to salvage from the bits and pieces gathered along the shore's edge.

The following are ruminations jotted down in the late hours, after the world has gone to sleep and the lessons of the day emerge.

Wasting Away

The moments of silence are gone. We run from them into the rush of unimportant things, so filled is the quiet with the painful whispers of all that goes unspoken. Busy-ness is our drug of choice, numbing our minds just enough to keep us from dwelling on all that we fear we can't change.

A compilation of coping mechanisms, we have become our fatigue. Unwilling or unable to cut ourselves free of this modern machine we have built, we're dragged in its wake all too quickly toward our end.

The virtue of a society's culture is reflected in the physical, mental, and emotional health of its people.

The time has come to part ways with all that is toxic, and preserve our quality of life.

Experience

Stop.
Go out.
Be the explorer of nights;
the inspector of storms;
the witness of the dawn.
You're breathing,
but how much of this life
have you actually lived?

The Weight

How strange that we should wait to act; that we should refrain from speaking our mind; that we should deny ourselves what we need.

In the end, the reasons that held us back are forgotten. The only thing we carry with us is the regret of all that went undone.

Lessons Learned

Beware the God who seeks praise. Beware the guru who presumes to teach that which is unfixed and boundless. Beware the healer who sets a price on aid. Beware the lover who would make you a lesser version of yourself. Beware the doctrines that discourage independent thought. Beware any person of faith who doesn't understand doubt.

Filter all things through yourself.
Accept only that which
sits right with your soul.

The Evolution of the Search

In the beginning we seek *truth.*
In the middle we seek *reason.*
In the end we seek *peace.*

Absorbing Organic Truth

There is an immortal one who exists, eternally speaking—
streaming—its collected wisdom, who can only be heard by
those who wade into the silence and listen.

Presence

The divine is in the present and you must be present to experience it. When you vacate the present and recede into your mind, allowing worries or work to remove you from the moment, you leave the plain upon which the divine dwells.

When you are constantly under the anesthetic of digital distraction, you withdraw; you are no longer conscious, and therefore are in no fit state to commune with the sacred.

If you wish to hear the answers you seek, you must be present to hear them. If you wish to partake in the insights there to be known, you must be present to receive them. If you wish to know the divine, you must be present to meet it.

...you must be present.

Meaningful Priorities

Take all those things that would propose to be important, and weigh them upon the scale of your soul. Asking how much each thing actually impacts, not just the moment, but the years ahead. Discard all that is trivial masquerading as significant, and reserve your days for those things that truly matter.

The Neglected Present

One day this will all be gone—these bones will be a fine dust churning in the morning breeze; the beams at the heart of this house will decay; the pages of this book will yellow, decompose, and yield the voice poured into them unto the mute expanse of sentiments forgotten.

Knowing the mortality of all things, I am left to hope that the emotions carried within this soul will be allowed to endure, and come with me to wherever fate shall next bid me to go. If they are not—if the soul's memory shall be lost in addition to all else—then life will have always been the present moment, and we will have lost so much of it to the regrets of the past and the worries of the future.

There is a balance to be struck between reaching for more and, at the same time, appreciating every ounce of what we have. Visualize what could be, but do not allow yourself to go blind to the dearness of what already *is*.

The Necessity of Solitude

Who are we without our addictions; without our media-induced hungers? So often the voices we hear echoing in our mind are not our own but that of our influencers. Isolation, while arguably going against human nature, is essential for mental and emotional health. Solitude is a detoxification of all that distorts our personality and misguides our path in life. It allows us to filter out the foreign opinions and hear our own voice—reach our authentic character—and practice fidelity to self.

The Nature of Our Relief

We all have those things that help us carry on through life. It is important that these things upon which we depend for daily strength are healthy for our character rather than harmful. We must ask ourselves whether the comforts we reach for each day are vices or virtues? Do they feed the best parts of us or do they rob us of them? Even when we are at our most fatigued and are tempted to reach for self-destructive things, we must try to seek out and take solace in those things that will lead to our eventual renewal; rather than those things that will only serve to bring us lower.

The Ineffable Journey

Realization is not transferable. While we may craft words to carry the truth learned in an effort to share our knowledge with others, we can neither impart the journey we took to our realizations nor the emotional resonance the truth had the moment it rippled through our life. We—each of us—must make our own journey to the truth. Only then will we have an emotional connection to the knowledge and possess an appreciation for why we believe what we do. In order for our beliefs to have any real power in shaping our character and actions, we must have an emotional mooring to them—such an anchor is forged over our journey unto that moment of clarity. Without the journey, knowledge is words, not revelation.

We cannot show each other the way; we can only spark in one another the desire to make the journey. We cannot teach one another anything; we can only awaken in one another the desire to teach ourselves. We cannot force each other to do good; we can only awaken in others the desire to *be* good. Then and only then is there lasting change.

The Fountain

We must seek out that which invigorates us, and engage it at all fronts. Art, music, literature, conversation, travel, nature—whatever it is that keeps the fire of our spirit bright—we must build our life around it; for, without our passions, the years ahead become a burden rather than a gift.

The Purpose of Boredom

Boredom is feared like the plague. We bury our head in busy-ness to avoid it, only serving to bring about an existential emptiness that we fear worse, when in actuality boredom is essential for creativity. It is a moment of calm wherein we can begin to reach for that new thing we have not yet conceived of.

To Look into the Mirror

From time to time, we all must go unto a landscape—be it inner or outer landscape—where there are no hiding places. Allowing the stark awe and silence to aid us in both communing and confronting the depth of ourselves.

We fear emptiness because we know that within those places of nothingness we will come face-to-face with who we are and gaze into the internal mirror. But what is the alternative? Shall we go our entire life without hearing our own voice . . . without ever having met who we are when isolated from all?

Know thy Self

There are so many things that distort our character. Fatigue, emptiness, anger, trauma, illness, addiction, the media... So many things are pulling on us—twisting us to become someone we are not. When we achieve balance and are at peace within ourselves, we are not affected by the pulling of the distortive forces at work. We need to achieve balance if for no other reason than we can finally be free of it all and can at last know who we are.

Allow the Infinite to be Infinite

Life doesn't have a singular purpose and yet we try to pigeonhole this infinite gift by searching for a single meaning behind our existence. We hunger for meaning the way a starving man does food—convinced we will waste away without it. As though to experience what it is to be alive weren't enough to justify drawing breath. Life is a multi-layered practice in exploration, self-definition, connection, and realization.

The greatest challenge presented to us as human beings is to allow the infinite to be infinite; to accept that we will always be the student never the teacher, and allow the truths we've gathered to evolve because what we seek to understand is a living thing and is in a perpetual state of change. Humanity's progression of understanding is open-ended. Anyone who professes mastery only shows their ignorance of the infinite procession of enlightenment of which they are a part. Each of us get to add a line into the coverless tome of understanding, which has no beginning and no end.

Full Circle

The path is a circle taking us from the place where we all begin, through the world, and then back to the beginning again. The journey would seem fruitless if it were not for the fact that, when we once again arrive home, we understand all that we didn't when we began, and see everything to which we were once blind.

Simplicity

There are days when life is complex and I require some answer to the how's and whys that surround the mysterious forces at work in my life. And still there are days when life is simple, and all I need is a heavy coat to wrap around me, a sturdy pair of boots, and a bag big enough to carry my load.

There are those days when, emptied by the hardships to befall me, I require a great deal for happiness. Those dark days when the worth of being alive eludes me in my haze of weariness. But then there are those moments when small joys bring a soothing warmth to my numb heart. Those days when my suffering recedes, the gray curtain rolls back, and the beauty of what it is to draw breath pervades. Those days of gratitude, appreciation, and simplicity.

The Cure

The cure for what ails is not to be found in a capsule. Our renewal must instead come from *within*. Synthetics are administered to the body yet they cannot reinforce the heart or re-weave the fibers of the fraying mind.

The cure for our modern maladies is dirt under the fingernails, and the feel of cool grass between the toes. The cure for our listlessness is to be out within the invigorating wind. The cure for our uselessness is to take up our stewardship of the earth; for it is not that there has been no work to be done, we simply have not been attending to it.

The Virtue of Doubt

Often, we do not come to our faith personally; rather, it is handed down to us by our parents, mentors, or our community. Accepting a set of truths that we have never personally tested is hazardous. Not only do we have no reasons for believing what we do, beyond the fact that others told us to do so, but we have taken as truth that which could be false.

There is a taboo around questioning tradition or long-held doctrine, but we must dare to do so. We mustn't fear being Godless for a time. We mustn't fear exploring the possibility that we are wrong. Periods of redefinition are healthy and necessary. Like a controlled burn in a forest that rids disease and encourages new growth.

One who has doubts simply requires the truth to prove itself. In the light of how abundant and convincing lies are in this age, doubt is not a weakness it is a form of *prudence*. Blind faith is dangerous; whereas doubt is cautious and educated.

Those teachers or communities that frown upon free-minded exchange do not show piety but *fear*—they fear that their own beliefs may be founded upon that which is false or perhaps that a hidden agenda will be revealed.

We cannot have confidence in our faith if our fidelity

to it is founded upon obligation or desperation. We cannot have what is genuine while clinging to what is false. Only two things can come from our doubting something: either our doubt turns out to be warranted and we leave behind a lie or we return to the truth with a justified certainty. So what is there to be feared? Doubt is a tool of redefinition that in turn leads to reaffirmation, devotion, and discovery.

We mustn't cling to our beliefs out of fear or complacency. We should either hold our beliefs confidently, or question them until we find the clarity required. When we take a faith in desperation, we will never know if what we believe is true or we simply *need* it to be.

For some, religion is a refuge, for others a foundation. Yet it often is used as a blanket we pull over our heads to protect us from the lurking monster of emptiness that we fear to face. Let your belief be composed of those few unalterable truths that neither time nor troubles are able to wear upon.

Question everything—no matter how beloved, or how long-held, or how exalted—without apology. Only those who build their world upon lies need fear an inquisitive mind. The truth will remain, even after a storm of doubt and revolution has washed over it. Only illusions need be protected. The truth need not be defended; it existed before us and will continue to exist after us.

Deus ex Machina

Evil demons dwelling in underworlds, Gods sitting on-high, angels battling and protecting. We have become so wrapped up in these stories, and in the in-fighting between the different religions, that the reality of the matter has gone unseen and unresolved.

We—humanity—must move out of this adolescence, put down the fairy tales, and take responsibility for our actions. There is no devil to blame, and there is no God to plead to. There is simply you and the choices you make each day—choices that will either make you a force of good in this world or an ill-presence.

People are the evil in this world, and likewise we are the divine. "Evil"—all that is detrimental to humanity—has come about as a result of poor choices and, by the same hand, the divine—the immortal goodness—endures as a result of loving, compassionate choices.

Heaven is created here—on this earth—by a community of compassionate people, and Hell is created here—on this earth—by a community of greedy, self-centered, apathetic people.

Our small choices define the greater picture.

Intimacy without Interference

Since my curiosity concerning *the great mystery* first emerged, I have believed that we are meant to gather an understanding of the divine from firsthand experience. While I hold a reverence for the wisdom of the past, I do not believe that insights of previous generations should go unscrutinized or unprogressed. Knowledge cannot be set in stone; for it is ever-evolving. Blind acceptance of unprogressed insight leads to a morally and spiritually stunted population. Such rigid thinking leaves us with religions that cling to outdated ideals and struggle to find their relevancy in a progressing world.

It is my belief that if we follow the heedings of our heart—follow the best instincts of our soul—we will be led to the answers we are in need of. Every soul is born connected to the divine—the immortal sacredness from which we came—and through that connection we can come to appreciate the deeper unseen workings underlining our life, and the world around us.

We use religion as an interface between us and the divine. Yet, as children of the divine, we need no interface. We need only develop our ability to listen and live in a soul-oriented manner.

A Maturing of Faith

The time has come to mature our ideas of the sacred. To move beyond worship and simply live in a state of reverence; to stop bowing and instead embrace; to stop preaching and let our actions speak for us.

Religion is the *history* of the journey to the divine. Spirituality is the pursuit of the divine in *the present*. Religion is *theory*. Spirituality is *practice*. In religion one studies the history of mankind and God. While through spirituality—through building a faith without interface—one finds the divine in the present, and lives with it.

We must abandon the institutions of religion. Religion has become a political arena—a rallying point for fanatics—a self-righteous guise for the self-centered individual. Leave the institutions, and instead dwell as the embodiment of your faith. Let your actions reflect the doctrine of your faith.

We Orphans of the Divine

Belief is not based upon our *certainty* in the unseen element; rather, upon our passion to learn of it. Our life's momentum is propelled by our curiosity, without which we are becalmed—resigned that there is no magic left in the world, only the shallowness of what is seen on the surface.

No matter the religion under which we categorize ourselves, in our heart we each hold the same yearning to know the divine. We each seek the divine like orphaned children longing for the embrace of their lost parents. We look into the mirror, searching ourselves, trying to see some semblance of our parents—the divine within us.

The journey unto our sacred origins is one of discovering just how far the connection in our soul might stretch. As we long to meet the greater soul who dreamt the universe into being.

Work to be Done

Do not hold a lazy faith. Miracles are not spontaneous events we must wait for helplessly. Miracles are an achievement—a breakthrough accomplished by those who pushed themselves beyond what was thought possible while holding a belief in a better life. Get up off your knees, and roll up your sleeves.

Maintaining One's Self

Do not be so quick to make meaningless sacrifice. The progression of understanding is not about growth through senseless deprivation. It is about the pursuit of what nourishes us. It isn't about fasting. It is the willingness to starve for a time if it means being free from a toxic presence in our life. It is about the willingness to walk away from anything or anyone that doesn't encourage the best part of us.

Devotion to the divine is found in our devotion to our best self. Self health is the first step toward group health. When the individual is ailing the community becomes sickly. In maintaining our own well-being we maintain the strength, not only to contemplate the greater matters atop our daily duties, but to help those around us.

The Dawn, Dark Night of the Soul and the Days After

There are many individuals who have undergone a spiritual awakening only to feel abandoned by the divine in later years; however, it is not so. The spiritual experience simply changes. The spiritual euphoria of the initial awakening, wherein we discover that there is indeed something greater and that we are connected to it, eventually calms as the once-extraordinary becomes integrated into our daily life.

Choosing this new conscious life, brings about a new heightened state of awareness, which inevitably leads us to see, not only the good but the evil in existence. This course of dark revelations leads us through a period of suffering, which only compounds our feeling of abandonment. But we have not been abandoned, we have simply been awakened, and that awakening is running its full course. Being aware means seeing both the good and the bad—what should be and what *is.*

Rapturous in the beginning, this knowledge settles within us to become our foundation for living as we endeavor to extend the known boundaries of love, and understanding.

Awareness is a gift but, at the same time, ignorance is a choice. We all have the ability to call for an awakening. And we mustn't despair when the initial wonderment fades. It doesn't mean that we have been forsaken. To be equipped to move through life aware is a continued gift of enlightenment bestowed on us by a divine being who loves us, and wishes to see us flourish.

The Mid-Step
unto Comprehension

Belief acts as a temporary bridge when we are trying to accept something that seems incomprehensible. We use belief and simply accept the workings we cannot understand until the time comes when at last we comprehend.

The Seed

Dreams are the gestation of a future reality. We do not come into being fully formed; rather, we gather, build, and grow. So too our matured identity—what we will be and do in this life—grows as well. Our reality begins as aspiration—vague dreams that sharpen over time until at last tangible. In nourishing our dreams we enable our future self to be born. In protecting that which is still taking root, we allow beauty to enter, and flourish in this world.

Yearning for Home

We have forgotten where we came from yet we still yearn to return home. We emigrated into the modern but in the end, we are still a folk of the farm and forest.

We tried to dwell in this foreign world of high-rises and neon-lights yet it is not who we are.

So the time has come to go back. Our ambitions took us into the West, and now our homesickness shall return us to the East.

Gripped by a longing for something our soul once knew, we shall empty the cities and flock to the shores, whereupon we shall dwell on the strand, until the boat comes to bring us back home.

Within the soul lives knowledge that this mind was never taught. To learn who we are we must forget what we were *told,* and remember what we *knew.*

Unto the Edge

The purpose of a pilgrimage is about setting aside a long period of time in which the only focus is to be the matters of the soul. Many believe a pilgrimage is about going away but it isn't; it is about coming home. Those who choose to go on pilgrimage have already ventured away from themselves; and now set out in a longing to journey back to who they are.

Many a time we believe we must go away from all that is familiar if we are to focus on our inner well-being because we feel it is the only way to escape all that drains and distracts us, allowing us to turn inward and tend to what ails us. Yet we do not need to go to the edges of the earth to learn who we are, only the edges of ourself.

Only Known to the Traveler

The precise age of our soul is something only we as individuals can know. Few of us lead a single life. There are times when I find myself longing for some nameless thing—something my soul once knew that is no longer present.

I mourn for loved ones lost whose names and faces I cannot recall. I feel a pull towards places upon which I have never set foot in this body, but somehow still know intimately. And in these yearnings I experience whispers of my own unknown past.

I have learned over my path that the division between lifetimes can be drawn by many occurrences; sometimes by the death of the body, and sometimes by an evolution of the soul.

Many think that only the end of one's body can draw the line between lives, but many lifetimes can be lived over the span of a single body. Our feet can travel the same paths each day yet immeasurable distance can be crossed. The physical measures of miles and years exist yet the internal measures are what truly define the extent of what has been.

Eventually the measurements imposed by man are too limited, and only the heart can define what has been endured, what has been accomplished, the distance traveled, and how many lives have been lived.

Clarity in Darkness

I find I suffer from sensory overload. The speed of the daylight world deafens and overwhelms. Night is more to my pace—the solemn simplicity and the space for rumination. Life still possesses a sense of grace while drinking in the light of the moon, and exploring the quietness the night yields.

I make all pivotal decisions based upon the feeling I have in my gut at the end of the day—as I lay there staring at the ceiling, into the darkness; for it is there in the dark, when my senses are deprived of all distractions, that my feelings concerning my life's direction become clear.

Night invites contemplation. At night the roar of the churning modern machine hushes, our daily tasks are done, and our duties are set aside. In the dim light—away from the set parameters of what is possible and impossible, aspiration ignites and we follow it hoping it will lead us unto a better version of ourselves.

In the beginning, during their most fragile stage, new dreams are too delicate for daylight. They must gather strength in the dark where all things are possible. Only after a time spent in the soft womb of night's unspoken thoughts, can we bring our dreams with us into the day, and not lose them to the harsh light of scrutiny. Heed the voice that rises in the calm of night. It is your true self.

The Cost of the Digital Age

The pace of this modern age is not conducive to maintaining one's consciousness. Glued to our electronics, we are blind and deaf to the world around us. Run down by our long work days, we are too exhausted to think and too hurried to feel. The day ends in a haze of strained thoughts, numbness, and fatigue. And we rise the next morning only to start the cycle again.

In this age of distraction, if you desire to fritter away your life with empty diversions, there is an abundance of gadgets available to aid you. Quietness is a characteristic of ages gone by. Our generation is the one it died with. Connected to the virtual world, we ignore the presence of those in our home. One can only hope we will awaken to the need for balance before we look up from the screen to find our loved ones have gone, and our life has passed us by.

Parting with
Burdensome Heirlooms

We pass hatred and prejudice on to our children, as though they were heirlooms of humanity. We cling to traditions that keep us bound to a way of life that no longer works and arguably never has.

Those who can glean the wisdom of the old traditions, but put away the ignorance and prejudices interwoven into them by the generations to come before, have always played a vital role in our global community; though their actions are usually met with resistance. We—all of us—must be assured that change can come without loss of identity. There are certain things we can leave along the roadside without becoming less than we are—certain heirlooms that, when let go, free us to move forward into a healthier future.

Letting it End Here

Justified within ourselves that we have suffered more than others, we feel guiltless when we disregard those in front of us, be they our family, our co-workers, strangers we interact with during our daily business, or faceless masses in foreign lands.

There are those who transcend the bitter acts done unto them, declaring that the pain shall end with them. And then there are those who use the crimes committed against them as a free pass to commit crimes against others.

Wronged as we each have been, nothing gives us the right to disregard the fragility of another. We can and must halt the hate passing throughout this world. A hateful act done unto us can be absorbed and transcended or it can be re-projected, thus allowing its ill force to continue moving throughout the population.

We must work to transcend those hateful things already carried out upon each of us and in doing so prevent new acts of hate from being done. We must work to heal from the wounds already received and connect to a sense of consideration, to ensure that we do not pass along any of our pain to the generations as yet unburdened.

We must declare a general amnesty; we must forgive each other and in doing so find that we have been forgiven. We must put away our bitterness and extend an open hand.

Self-inflictive Tendencies

We veer towards the self-destructive, so willing to throw ourselves from the cliff of despair. In the end, I cannot help but wonder if we prefer to mourn the meaning our life lacks rather than cultivate that which will actually give us joyful purpose.

A little sorrow is harmless—a trickle of blood can remind us of our mortality—until it spreads to our entire being and, in a hemorrhage of self-pity, we lose all perspective. As a people, we have defined our emotional depth through explorations into agony.

In society the deep soul is the tormented one. When we want to feel, we gravitate towards those artists who let us witness their unraveling; however, it takes little effort to sink—to wantonly give ourselves to despondency and spill out our pain. We are so filled with it we have mistakenly come to believe it defines who we are.

It takes far more courage—considerably more effort—to tap into hope than into the despair. The fearless one bears, not the wounds on his heart but the love he still wishes to give.

It takes more depth of soul to believe life can be better than to give ourselves to despair and become a martyr to our own world-weariness.

The Lament

All grief is suffered upon an epic scale. When loss strikes, our world ends. There is no greater struggle than that of recovering from the apocalypse that is the death of one dear to us.

Having suffered my own losses and walked the long procession, I know there are no words to express the depth of mourning. It is a woebegone eternal night of oblivion unto madness. Our life is smashed against the rocks of a bitter sea and we are left gasping for breath between strangled sobs.

All we can do is come to a reckoning.

Let there be a promise between the lover and the lost that there shall indeed be a reunion and, once had, there shall be no next parting.

The Origin of Compassion

We believe that we can sell each other in order to escape our own poverty; that we can sell our life in order to live and not end up in debt. We believe that we can put each other down in order to climb out of our own insecurities. We believe that we can lash out at each other to overcome our own self-loathing. But what we must realize is that we are all interconnected and in hurting one another we only serve to further damage ourselves.

Where there is loss of self, there can be no growth. Where there is loss of morality, there can be no gain. Where there is loss of humanity, there can be no evolution. Where there is loss of ideals, there can be no progress.

Compassion has been said to be the answer. Yet what is this virtue possessed by the prophets and Buddhas? Compassion is the consideration we extend to a stranger. It is our attempt to understand another's pains, even though we do not know their history. It is a blind sympathy given unto all beings, even before we know what their personal plight may be. It is a baseline respect for the worth of another's life. It is the principle that says: We need not know someone before we are willing to extend some degree of love to them.

Compassion is a love that precedes personal connection. Once stories are exchanged and there is connection, compassion evolves into care. Compassion is what bridges the distance between ourselves and those we do not know. It is a baseline love for all beings that allows us to be understanding and considerate towards even those whom we do not know.

It is obvious that such an undiminished, un-biased love as compassion is needed within this world. The difficultly comes in tapping into such a source of love within ourselves. It seems an unrealistic ideal to believe any person can attain within them a love for all humanity that never diminishes; something achievable only by those saviors who possess none of humanity's weaknesses.

It is my conclusion that kindness does not always come *naturally*. In this age of fatigue, we always have an excuse to go cold unto those around us but, at the same time, there is never any excuse. Often, kindness is a *conscious choice* that we make—we *choose* to pull from ourselves compassion and we find we now have patient consideration whereas once we didn't.

In loving each other, we believe in each other's worth.

To Become Who We Are

The thing it takes the most strength to do is to change what we know to be wrong with our life. . . . To stop clinging to that which is detrimental. To stop ignoring the wrongness we partake in or condone. To walk away from the lover that we know to be harmful to us. To leave the job that wears away at our soul.

To stop wanting that which does not fill us. To stop going to those places where we do not belong. To stop acting on those self-destructive feelings and commit to strengthening what we know to be fragile within us. To stop doing the easy thing and start doing the needed thing. To stop ignoring the voice of our better-selves and become that strong authentic soul that is free of vices and the opinions of the mob. To become our belief, instead of indulging our despair. To become our ideals, instead of succumbing to our pessimism. To become our truth, instead of what others need us to be. To become what it is to be human, by bringing forth our humanity.

What We Each Must Do

Shall we not recover ourselves? Shall we not redeem ourselves to one another? Shall we not restore this world?

Could we not be the generation who did what always should have been done? Who took the *hard* path so that humanity could be returned to the *right* path? Shall we not reexamine all that we choose to pursue and reconsider what will actually fulfill us?

The past has been defined by what we have done; while the present and future are decided by what we choose to do.

Shall we believe in what should be and go in search of it? Shall we believe in what *needs to be* and build it together?

We become more by believing that we can be more. Life becomes better when we are willing to act on the belief that it can be better.

To believe is to reach and reach is what we all must do.

The Sacred Ordinary

Becoming aware of the dearness in what might otherwise be regarded as mundane is the ultimate form of insight.

Metamorphosis

It is time for a rebirth;
for the skin of the old life
can no longer contain who we are.

Afterword

Wild Silence
Seeking Solace in the Age of the Digital Din

"Simplify, simplify."
—HENRY DAVID THOREAU, *Walden*

Thoreau's celebrated urging has become a modern necessity. Now more than ever, we must fight to preserve our consciousness, and the health of our psyche.

To survive in this multi-track digital world that never ceases—never allows us a moment of rest—we must develop the ability to simplify in order to maintain physical and emotional well-being. Some aspects of our ever-hurried life must be slowed, or the pace will kill us. The wider the web, the less we stop to take in the horizon. Our mind, our body, and our spirit require that solace that stillness brings in order to regulate our mental and physical health.

When we give our focus to something, it is as though we are plugging our mind into it; we zero in and all else fades away. When we give our focus to the digital streams of work and media, we are plugging our minds into something draining, chaotic, and usually empty. And so we suffer mental fatigue after prolonged periods of overexposure to this world.

The cure for this mental strain is to focus on something soothing, simple, and profound. The most rejuvenating source of these restorative elements being the very world we vacated when entering the digital, and that is the still-wild places of the natural world. The tonic for an overburdened mind is to unplug from all that drains and bombards, and reconnect with the stillness and soothing cycles of nature. When you find yourself consumed in the unimportant and exhausted by the blinding pace, go unto the mountains and let the majesty bring you to a halt.

A Modern Pandemic: The Hysteria of Emptiness

We all have heard the virtues of meditation and mindfulness. We know deep within ourselves that we're clinging to unhealthy ways, but how do we change directions?

We are hurdling forward now, seemingly unable to stop ourselves from making that next great distraction, even though we all sense the heavy importance of just sitting quiet for a time, and addressing the ever-widening holes fraying along the seams of our soul.

We are, all of us, writhing in a silent hysteria of emptiness. No, we're not hysterical in the sense that we are running naked through the streets, sobbing, clawing at ourselves. Instead, the hysteria is a silent one, taking place as we are staring deadpan and milky-eyed into our screens; mainlining the anesthetic of our digital distractions, so afraid to face a single moment sober.

Is the hole within us insatiable? Can it be filled? Or is it simply a part of humanity's unseen anatomy? The person who holds a curiosity for the world has an intact hope that the hole can indeed be filled. This hope is what separates the mad ones from the sane.

To begin to address the holes in our life we must recognize what drives us each day. Being aware of your driving emotions helps you to pinpoint and defuse detrimental behavior. When I was younger, I was driven by *curiosity*. I went to books of philosophy, religion, literature, and verse looking for experience, for truth, for moments of awe, but at some point my driving emotions changed; desperation sprang up in the place of my dying curiosity. The nature of what I sought changed as well. I began reaching for distractions. My belief in answers and expectation of transcendent experience all but lost. Strong drinks, empty relationships, screens of fruitless interaction, extra projects at work—all things unimportant that possess that momentary numbing quality became my life, when they in no way reflected the virtuous and mindful character I so painstakingly defined in my youth.

The course I took from enthusiasm to avoidance is common to many. We routinely use unhealthy coping mechanisms to deal with stress, fatigue, and hopelessness. Ignoring the fact that we the nature of what we depend upon to get through the day is damaging and will only serve to bring us lower in the long run.

So where are we left—we who feel the emptiness but no longer have the fire of curiosity driving us? We can plug-in to the 24-hr media stream, and let it flow through our veins like propofol until the voice of our emptiness slurs into white noise. We can make our way across the stretching years before us by leaping from one distraction to another. Or we can take to the road and recapture what we have lost.

We can store up the energy to search as we once did— to rediscover that interest in life that lay at the heart of our curiosity.

Exhaustion of the soul is different than that of the body. Sleep doesn't restore strength to the soul nor does food; (at least, not the food we force-feed ourselves before punching a clock on a job we have no emotional stake in). What we need to recharge ourselves cannot be pinpointed; each source is specific to the individual. The search is something we each must do for ourselves.

To set out on this journey of restoration, we must first cast off as many weights as possible—toxic relations and detrimental coping mechanisms—and scale back work and digital distractions where possible. Next, we must free ourselves to take up the search by requiring less of the material world so that we need not sell as many hours of our life to sustaining our survival. Then, with the hours we have reclaimed, we must face our fears—face the silence. We must bring ourselves to sit with the only stranger in this life that we must come to know: ourselves. Sit there without vice or distraction and just *be*—be until the fits of boredom pass, the apparitions of the hungry ghosts are dispelled, and we find something worth knowing in the quiet.

We must sit and have tea with ourselves, settle in a deep chair in a café nestled in a town square, watching the stream of life and change go on, remembering that we too are a part of that change. The good shall pass so savor it. The bad shall likewise pass so don't dwell on it.

We must walk with ourselves along wooded paths soaking in the sunlight and silence through the open pores of our soul. We must fall asleep in the grass as we did when we were children allowing the warmth of the light to be our weightless blanket. We must travel and invigorate our senses—see the world from new angles, and shake off the fear of the unknown that comes with staying in too small a sphere for too long a time. We must stay home, and cook ourselves a meal from scratch. Sit down with a plate of ripened fruit and bread we kneaded with our hands and remember what it is to savor a moment in time. We must book a ticket on a train, sit by the window, and watch the landscape roll by—flat at first then rising up to the peaked mountains before sinking back down to the white-capped sea—and remember that the destination isn't important, it's the journey that is the gift. We are all going to the same place; it's how we choose to get there that defines the life we lead.

*　　*　　*

All that said, even now as you read these words and agree with the conclusions, how many will actually take them to heart? We are broken, yes, but it would seem for many the hole hasn't grown wide enough to spur us to change our detrimental ways. It would seem we prefer the crutch to the march; to limp along rather than run; to bemoan what might have been rather than do the work, and build what could be.

We all know what needs to be done. How many of us will choose to do it?

. . . At the end of this, you may think that I am preaching to you, but I'm not. I'm simply giving a louder voice to what your heart is already telling you, because my heart is telling me the same thing, and I've come to a point where I must listen.

About the Author

L.M. Browning grew up in a small fishing village in Connecticut. A longtime student of religion, nature, and philosophy these themes permeate her work. She is the author of a three-title contemplative poetry series *Oak Wise, Ruminations at Twilight*, and *The Barren Plain*. These books went on to garner several accolades including a total of 3 pushcart-prize nominations and the Nautilus Gold Medal for Poetry. In 2012, she released *Fleeting Moments of Fierce Clarity: Journal of a New England Poet*, which went on to be named a finalist in the Next Generation Indie Book Awards. Then, in 2013, she released her novel *The Nameless Man*.

Balancing her passion for writing with her love of education and publishing, Browning is a graduate of the University of London and a Fellow with the League of Conservationist Writers. She is Partner at Hiraeth Press, Co-Founder of *Written River*, and Founder of *The Wayfarer*. In 2011, Browning opened Homebound Publications--a rising independent publishing house based in New England. She is currently working to complete a B.A. at Harvard University's Extension School in Cambridge, Massachusetts. Her next novel *The Castoff Children* will be released in the autumn of 2016.

www.lmbrowning.com

HOMEBOUND
PUBLICATIONS

At Homebound Publications we publish books written by soul-oriented individuals putting forth their works in an effort to restore depth, highlight truth, and improve the quality of living for their readers.

As an independent publisher we strive to ensure that "the mainstream is not the only stream." With the release of each book, we aim to introduce new perspectives that will directly aid mankind in the trials we face at present as a global village.

So often in this age of commerce, entertainment supersedes growth; books of lesser integrity but higher marketability are chosen over those with much-needed truth but a smaller audience. We focus on the quality of the truth and insight present before any other considerations.

At Homebound Publications we value authenticity and fresh ideas. From the submissions process where we choose our projects right down to the crafting of each finished book, our intention is to provide a moment of solace and insight for our readers.

CPSIA information can be obtained at www.ICGtesting.com
Printed in the USA
BVOW05s1745190815

413968BV00001B/1/P